GIANT CHRISTMAS FUN BOOK

DOVER PUBLICATIONS, INC.
Mineola, New York

Note

Celebrate the Christmas season with this giant book full of festive activities. You can start off by adding color to thirty black-and-white illustrations of the Cat family, as they act out scenes from the classic tale *The Night Before Christmas* (pages 1–32). Next (pages 33–64), you get to complete a series of challenging puzzles and activities, ranging from dot-to-dots, to mazes, crossword puzzles, and more—each of which feature Christmas characters and cheer. If you get stuck, solutions for this section can be found beginning on page 59. It wouldn't be Christmas without Christmas cookies—and the coloring book found on pages 65–96 is about just that! Color the pictures of Molly and Jack as they bake a batch of the yummiest Christmas cookies ever, and take a peek at their special recipes at the end! For a challenging Christmas activity, turn to pages 97–144, where you'll get to search for hidden pictures in cute and chaotic Christmas scenes. Solutions for this section can be found beginning on page 136. Some traditional Christmas coloring can be found on pages 145–176, where a host of yuletide traditions have been artistically rendered into festive holiday patterns and abstract designs. Highlights include gingerbread men, nutcracker dolls, ornaments, candles, Santa Claus, and more. Continue coloring through pages 177–208, where you can add your own artistic touch to pictures of Ben, Emmie, and the rest of their family as they get ready to celebrate the Christmas season. Follow them as they count down the days, go Christmas shopping, put up the tree and hang the lights, write letters to Santa, and wake up on Christmas morning. Finally, on pages 209–270 practice drawing a host of holiday images— Rudolph, Christmas trees, gingerbread men, snowflakes, and of course, Santa Claus! There is so much to do inside this book, it'll keep you busy through the whole holiday season! Have fun!

Bibliographical Note

Giant Christmas Fun Book, first published in 2013, contains the following seven previously published Dover Books: *The Night Before Christmas* by Clement Clarke Moore, illustrated by Anna Pomaska (2000), *Christmas Puzzle Fun* by Becky Radtke (2005), *How to Draw Christmas Pictures* by Barbara Soloff Levy (2005), *Christmas Family Fun Coloring Book* by Cathy Beylon (2006), *Christmas Find & Color* by Agostino Traini (2009), *ChristmasScapes* by Jessica Mazurkiewicz (2009), and *Color & Cook CHRISTMAS COOKIES* by Monica Wellington (2009).

International Standard Book Number

ISBN-13: 978-0-486-49176-9
ISBN-10: 0-486-49176-5

Manufactured in the United States by Courier Corporation
49176501   2013
www.doverpublications.com

The Night Before Christmas

Clement Clarke Moore

Illustrated by
Anna Pomaska

'Twas the night before Christmas,
when all through the house,

Not a creature was stirring, not even a mouse;

The stockings were hung by the chimney with care,
In hopes that St. Nicholas soon would be there;

The children were nestled all snug in their beds,

While visions of sugarplums danced in their heads;

And Mamma in her 'kerchief and I in my cap,
Had just settled our brains for a long winter's nap.

When out on the lawn there arose such a clatter,
I sprang from the bed to see what was the matter.

Away to the window I flew like a flash,
Tore open the shutters and threw up the sash.

The moon on the breast of the new-fallen snow,
Gave lustre of mid-day to objects below.

11

When, what to my wondering eyes should appear,
But a miniature sleigh, and eight tiny reindeer.

12

With a little old driver, so lively and quick,
I knew in a moment it must be St. Nick.

More rapid than eagles his coursers they came,
And he whistled, and shouted,
and called them by name;

14

"Now, *Dasher!* Now, *Dancer!* Now, *Prancer* and *Vixen!*
On, *Comet!* On, *Cupid!* On, *Donner* and *Blitzen!*

15

To the top of the porch! to the top of the wall!
Now dash away! dash away! dash away all!"

As dry leaves that before the wild hurricane fly,
When they meet with an obstacle, mount to the sky;
So up to the house-top the coursers they flew,
With the sleigh full of toys,
and St. Nicholas, too.

17

And then, in a twinkling, I heard on the roof
The prancing and pawing of each little hoof—

As I drew in my head, and was turning around,
Down the chimney St. Nicholas came with a bound!

He was dressed all in fur, from his head to his foot,
And his clothes were all tarnished
with ashes and soot.

A bundle of toys he had flung on his back,
And he looked like a peddler just opening his pack.

His eyes—how they twinkled!
His dimples—how merry!
His cheeks were like roses, his nose like a cherry!

His droll little mouth
was drawn up like a bow,
And the beard of his chin
was as white as the snow;
The stump of a pipe
he held tight in his teeth,
And the smoke it encircled
his head like a wreath;
He had a broad face
And a little round belly,
That shook when he laughed,
Like a bowlful of jelly.

He was chubby and plump, a right jolly old elf,
And I laughed when I saw him, in spite of myself,

A wink of his eye and a twist of his head,
Soon gave me to know I had nothing to dread;

25

He spoke not a word, but went straight to his work,
And fill'd all the stockings; then turned with a jerk,

And laying his finger aside of his nose,
And giving a nod, up the chimney he rose;

He sprang to his sleigh, to his team gave a whistle,

And away they all flew like the down of a thistle.

But I heard him exclaim, ere he drove out of sight,

To: Mouse
From: Santa,
with love

Christmas Puzzle Fun

Becky Radtke

Door Decoration

Connect the dots in order from 1 to 50 to see something many people hang on their outside doors during the holiday season.

Holiday Hunt

Below are some words that we often hear at Christmastime. See if you can find and circle them all in this letter grid. Look carefully—they are hidden vertically, horizontally, diagonally and backwards.

snow	cookies	bows	Santa
carols	North Pole	reindeer	sleigh
bells	mistletoe	stocking	tree
elf	ornament	present	holly

I see one!

```
A P R E S E N T H S W Q H J N
B R U O D L Q Z A O Z P S R O
M E E R T O H T N D L E M P R
S I K N B J N S Y R T L G M T
I N Z A G A X C K L B F Y H H
P D T M S R C A R O L S K I P
T E J E K Q O S L E I G H S O
Z E C N D W O M E Y S O Q L L
U R S T O C K I N G D W R L E
E Y P M E V I Q U Y J N O E N
L E N V N K E X L T O X Z B S
E O T E L T S I M J Y M B Y Z
```

Frosty Friend

Use the words on the mittens below to fill in the blanks in this verse. The completed poem tells about a fun holiday activity.

Make a great big _____,

Put another one on that . . .

Then place a small one for the _____

And add a black top hat!

Use two buttons for the _____,

Stick a carrot nose in place . . .

Press on a red yarn _____

To complete this happy face!

Find branches for the _____,

And at last the work is done!

Now you have a frosty _____

To join the Christmas fun!

head   friend   eyes

smile   arms   snowball

Trimmed Tree

Decorating a Christmas tree can be lots of fun! Determine which tree Jason and his family just trimmed by reading these clues . . .

A. It has ornaments on it.

B. It has a star on top.

C. It has gifts under it.

Jason's tree is number _____.

Christmas Cookies

Eddie Elf has been baking Christmas cookies, but he has just run out of some important ingredients. Find out what he needs by unscrambling the words below.

i m k l

_____

a l s t

_____

l i a v n l a

_____

n i r s s i a

_____

u l r o f

_____

g e s g

_____

r g u s a

_____

u s n t

_____

n m n n o c i a

_____

k g n a i b   a o d s

_____

Shopping Spree

Kelly is buying Christmas presents for her family and friends. Find out what's in her bag by using the picture clues to fill in the crossword puzzle below.

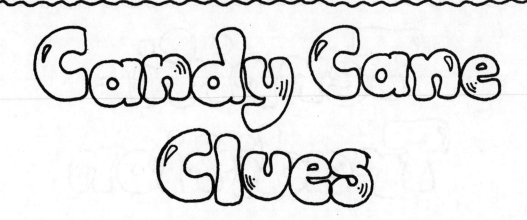

Candy Cane Clues

Read the clues to help you determine which candy cane belongs to Debbie.

A.) It is big.
B.) It has stripes.
C.) It has a bow tied around it.
D.) It has a small piece missing.

Candy cane number _____ belongs to Debbie.

Terrific Tradition

Josh and his friends like to do a certain thing every year around Christmas. You can find out what it is by writing the words on the music sheets onto the blanks that match their numbers.

Beautiful Bells

Use a crayon or pencil to cross out the first bell. Then continue to cross out every second bell after that. The remaining letters will spell out a merry message!

Odd Ornaments

Jennifer has taken these ornaments out of a box in the attic. Try finding and circling the six that are exactly the same.

Puzzling Picture

Discover the hidden Christmas picture below by coloring it according to the shape code given.

Color all ▲ 's red.

Color all ■ 's yellow.

Color all ● 's purple.

Color all ♥ 's green.

Color all ★ 's blue.

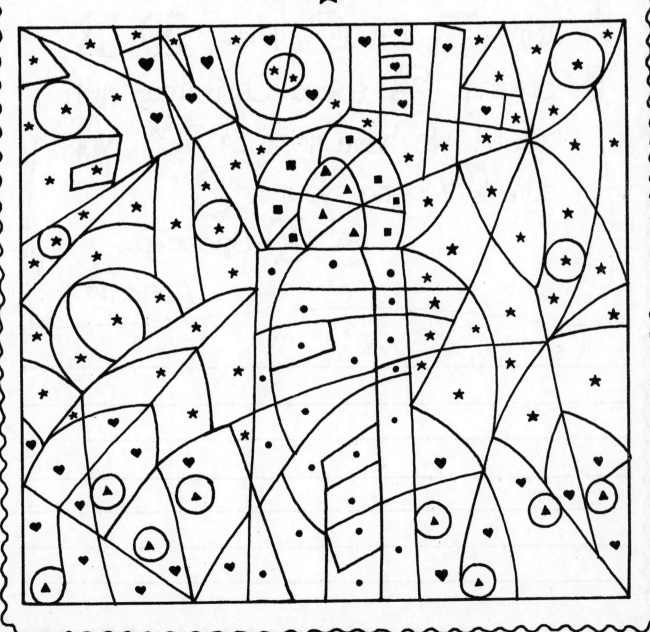

Neat Note

Someone has written this note in a silly sort of way. See if you can figure out what it says by writing it out at the bottom of the page, replacing pictures and large letters and numbers with words they sound like, and subtracting letters where indicated (i.e. "hat-h" = "at").

Dear 🦆,

👁 M so 😊 that U R coming 2 spend Christmas with bus-b! We have tons of ❄❄. 🐝 sure U bring your ⛸! C U Spoon-p,

Ann + D

_____

_____

_____

_____

_____

_____

_____

Different Doll

Santa's elves have just made these dolls. They should all be the same, but they aren't. Draw a rectangle around the different doll.

Word Workout

Put on your thinking cap and see how many different five-letter words you can write using the letters in "Merry Christmas." No plurals allowed! (The answers given are only some of the possible words.)

Merry Christmas

Guess My Gift

Each of these children is hoping for a special Christmas present. To find out what they want, replace each letter of their thoughts with the letter preceding it in the alphabet (the whole alphabet is shown in the gift box below).

A B C D E F G H I J K L M
N O P Q R S T U V W X Y Z

T L B U F C P B S E
_ _ _ _ _ _ _ _ _

Q V Q Q Z
_ _ _ _ _

C J D Z D M F
_ _ _ _ _ _ _

W J E F P   H B N F
_ _ _ _ _   _ _ _ _

Same Santas

Get your pencil sharpened, then finish drawing Santa number two so that he looks just like Santa number one.

Ready Reindeer

Santa's magic reindeer are all ready for their big flight! Fill in the blanks with a D, R, C or I to spell their names. Then shout them out one by one so they'll take off!

ASHE

ANCE

P_AN_E_

V_XEN

_OMET

_UP__

ONNE

BL_TZEN

Fantastic Forecast

Santa and Mrs. Claus want to know what the weather will be like for Christmas Eve. The weather forecaster on the television is giving a report, but all of her words are spelled backwards. Write them correctly onto the blanks to find out what she is saying.

samtsirhC evE thgin lliw eb

_____ ___ _____ ____ __

yrev dloc. tI lliw wons ffo

____ ____ __ ____ ____ ___

dna no tuohguorht eht gnineve.

___ __ _____ ___ _____

Super Stocking

Print your name on this stocking, then color and decorate it any way you'd like. Finally, draw some items coming out of the top that you want to find in your stocking Christmas morning.

Help the Helpers

Santa wants his helpers to work in pairs. Draw a line to connect each pair of elves whose names rhyme.

Bumbles

Sporty

Blinky

Winky

Giggles

Doodles

Noodles

Fumbles

Shorty

Wiggles

Tons of Toys

Santa's elves are busy in the workshop making all kinds of toys. You can help them by finishing the toys below. (Using the grid lines as a guide, copy the shown features in mirror-image across the center of each picture.)

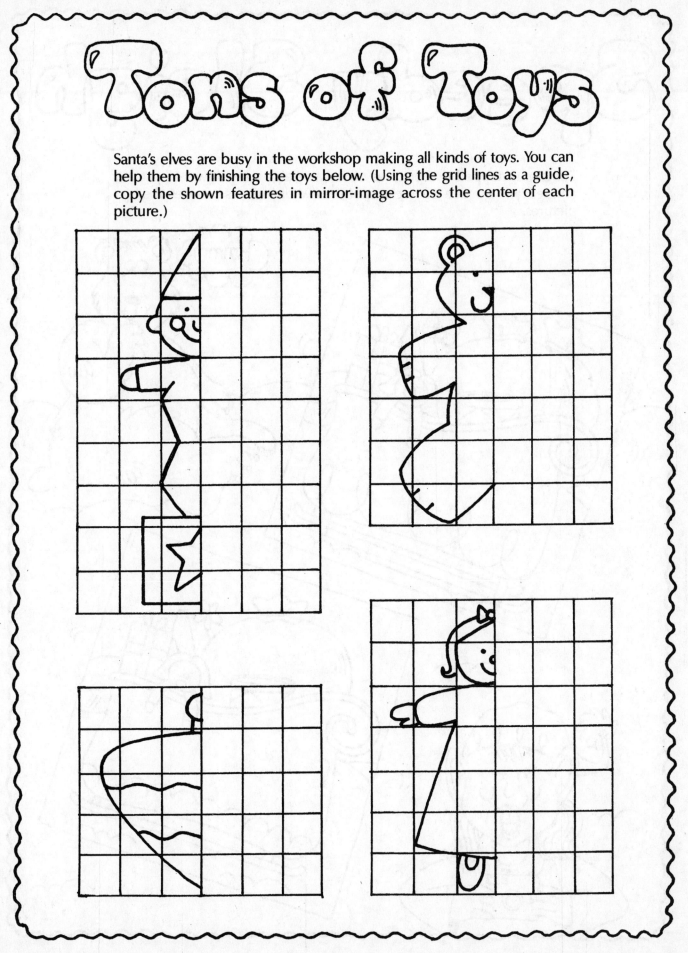

Speedy Sleigh

Someone snapped two pictures of Santa's sleigh when it was all packed and ready to go. See if you can spot the five differences between the two pictures.

Robby Reindeer

Follow these five easy steps to learn how to draw "Robby Reindeer."

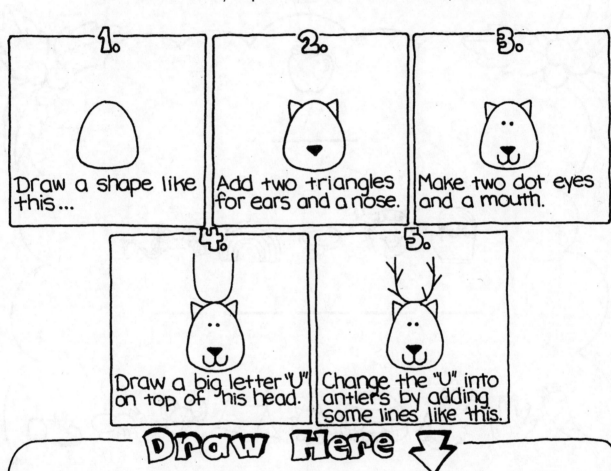

1. Draw a shape like this...

2. Add two triangles for ears and a nose.

3. Make two dot eyes and a mouth.

4. Draw a big letter "U" on top of his head.

5. Change the "U" into antlers by adding some lines like this.

Draw Here ⬇

Warm Wish

Write the first letter of each pictured item onto the blank below it. When you are done you will find out what we hope you will have!

____

__ __ __ __ __

__ __ __ __ __ __ __ __ __

and
a Happy New Year

SOLUTIONS

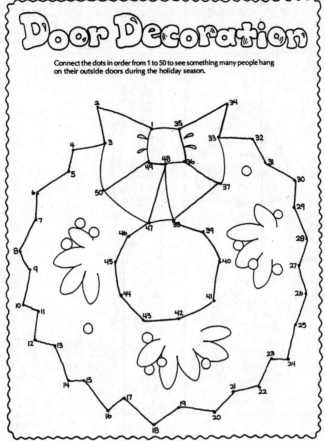

Door Decoration

Connect the dots in order from 1 to 50 to see something many people hang on their outside doors during the holiday season.

Holiday Hunt

Below are some words that we often hear at Christmastime. See if you can find and circle them all in this letter grid. Look carefully—they are hidden vertically, horizontally, diagonally and backwards.

snow	cookies	bows	Santa
carols	North Pole	reindeer	sleigh
bells	mistletoe	stocking	tree
elf	ornament	present	holly

I see one!

```
A P R E S E N T H S W Q H J N
B R U O D L Q Z A O Z P S J R
M E E R T O H T N D L E M P O
S I K N B J N S Y R T L G M H
I N Z A G A X C K L B F Y H T
P D E T J M S R C A R O L S K
T E J E K Q O S L E I G H S I
Z E C N D W O M E Y S Q Q L O
U R S T O C K I N G D W R L L
E Y P M E V I Q U Y J N O E E
L E N V N K E X L T O X Z B S
E O T E L T S I M J Y M B Y Z
```

Frosty Friend

Use the words on the mittens below to fill in the blanks in this verse. The completed poem tells about a fun holiday activity.

Make a great big <u>snowball</u>,
Put another one on that . . .
Then place a small one for the <u>head</u>
And add a black top hat!
Use two buttons for the <u>eyes</u>,
Stick a carrot nose in place . . . .
Press on a red yarn <u>smile</u>
To complete this happy face!
Find branches for the <u>arms</u>,
And at last the work is done!
Now you have a frosty <u>friend</u>
To join the Christmas fun!

head   friend   eyes
smile   arms   snowball

Trimmed Tree

Decorating a Christmas tree can be lots of fun! Determine which tree Jason and his family just trimmed by reading these clues . . .

A. It has ornaments on it.
B. It has a star on top.
C. It has gifts under it.

Jason's tree is number 4.

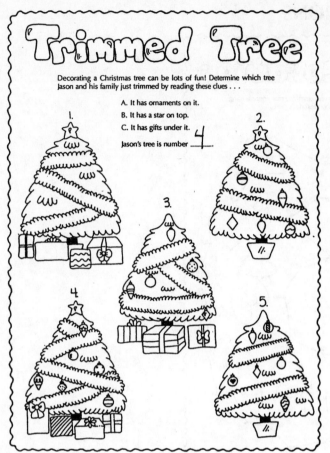

Christmas Cookies

Eddie Elf has been baking Christmas cookies, but he has just run out of some important ingredients. Find out what he needs by unscrambling the words below.

i m k l
milk

a l s t
salt

l i a v n l a
vanilla

n i r s s i a
raisins

u l r o f
flour

g e s g
eggs

r g u s a
sugar

u s n t
nuts

n m n n o c i a
cinnamon

k g n a i b
baking

a o d s
soda

Shopping Spree

Kelly is buying Christmas presents for her family and friends. Find out what's in her bag by using the picture clues to fill in the crossword puzzle below.

Candy Cane Clues

Read the clues to help you determine which candy cane belongs to Debbie.

A.) It is big.
B.) It has stripes.
C.) It has a bow tied around it.
D.) It has a small piece missing.

Candy cane number 5 belongs to Debbie.

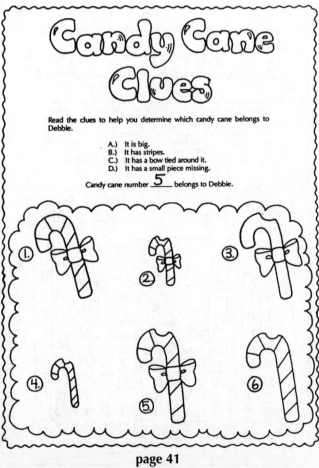

Terrific Tradition

Josh and his friends like to do a certain thing every year around Christmas. You can find out what it is by writing the words on the music sheets onto the blanks that match their numbers.

THEY   GO   FROM   HOUSE   TO
1.   2.   3.   4.   5.
HOUSE   SINGING   CHRISTMAS   CAROLS .
6.   7.   8.   9.

page 42

Beautiful Bells

Use a crayon or pencil to cross out the first bell. Then continue to cross out every second bell after that. The remaining letters will spell out a merry message!

page 43

Odd Ornaments

Jennifer has taken these ornaments out of a box in the attic. Try finding and circling the six that are exactly the same.

page 44

Neat Note

Someone has written this note in a silly sort of way. See if you can figure out what it says by writing it out at the bottom of the page, replacing pictures and large letters and numbers with words they sound like, and subtracting letters where indicated (i.e. "hat-h" = "at").

Dear 🐝,
👁 M so 😊 that U R
coming 2 spend Christmas with
bus-b! We have tons of ❄. 🐝
sure U bring your ⛸!
C U Spoon-p,
Ann + D

Dear Bill,
I am so happy that you are coming to spend Christmas with us! We have tons of snow. Be sure you bring your ice skates!
See you soon,
Andy

page 46

61

Different Doll

Santa's elves have just made these dolls. They should all be the same, but they aren't. Draw a rectangle around the different doll.

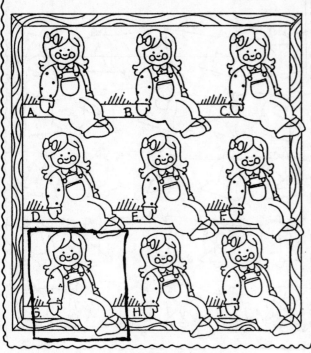

page 47

Word Workout

Put on your thinking cap and see how many different five-letter words you can write using the letters in "Merry Christmas." No plurals allowed! (The answers given are only some of the possible words.)

Merry Christmas

heart	messy
steam	smash
match	itchy
miser	marsh
chime	smear
yeast	charm
stare	marry
chart	shirt
carry	cream
scram	mirth
arise	smart

page 48

Guess My Gift

Each of these children is hoping for a special Christmas present. To find out what they want, replace each letter of their thoughts with the letter preceding it in the alphabet (the whole alphabet is shown in the gift box below).

A B C D E F G H I J K L M
N O P Q R S T U V W X Y Z

T L B U F C P B S E
SKATEBOARD

Q V Q Q Z
PUPPY

C J D Z D M E
BICYCLE

W J E F P H B N F
VIDEO GAME

page 49

Ready Reindeer

Santa's magic reindeer are all ready for their big flight! Fill in the blanks with a D, R, C or I to spell their names. Then shout them out one by one so they'll take off!

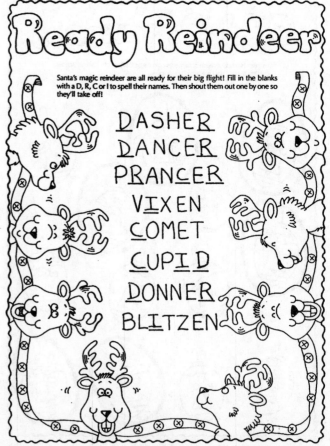

DASHER
DANCER
PRANCER
VIXEN
COMET
CUPID
DONNER
BLITZEN

page 51

Fantastic Forecast

Santa and Mrs. Claus want to know what the weather will be like for Christmas Eve. The weather forecaster on the television is giving a report, but all of her words are spelled backwards. Write them correctly onto the blanks to find out what she is saying.

samtsirhC evE thgin lliw eb
Christmas Eve night will be
yrev dloc. +I lliw wons ffo
very cold. It will snow off
dna no tuohguorht eht gnineve.
and on throughout the evening.

page 52

Help the Helpers

Santa wants his helpers to work in pairs. Draw a line to connect each pair of elves whose names rhyme.

Bumbles Sporty Blinky

Winky Giggles Ha Ha Ha Ha Noodles

Doodles

Fumbles Shorty Wiggles

page 54

Speedy Sleigh

Someone snapped two pictures of Santa's sleigh when it was all packed and ready to go. See if you can spot the five differences between the two pictures.

Hmmm...

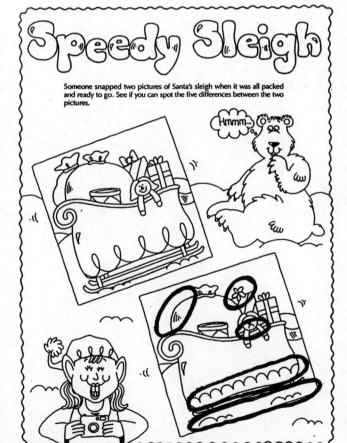

page 56

Warm Wish

Write the first letter of each pictured item onto the blank below it. When you are done you will find out what we hope you will have!

A

MERRY

CHRISTMAS

and

a Happy New Year

page 58

MONICA WELLINGTON

Molly and Jack are playing in the snow.
It's a wintry day and Christmas is coming soon!

It's a day to get ready for Christmas. Jack and Molly decorate the tree.

It's a day for baking cookies!
Jack and Molly choose a recipe in their favorite holiday cookbook.

Molly and Jack are getting ready to make Christmas sugar cookies.

Christmas baker's hat

apron with a candycane

rolling pin

cookie cutters

mixing bowl

plastic measuring cups

wooden spoon

cookie trays

FLOUR

1 DOZEN EGGS

BUTTER

measuring spoons

timer

potholder

SUGAR

MILK

Vanilla

Baking Powder

Salt

spatula

Can you help find all of the utensils and ingredients that they need?

Jack and Molly want to make a lot of cookies, so they make two batches of cookie dough. They each have a big bowl and measure out their ingredients.

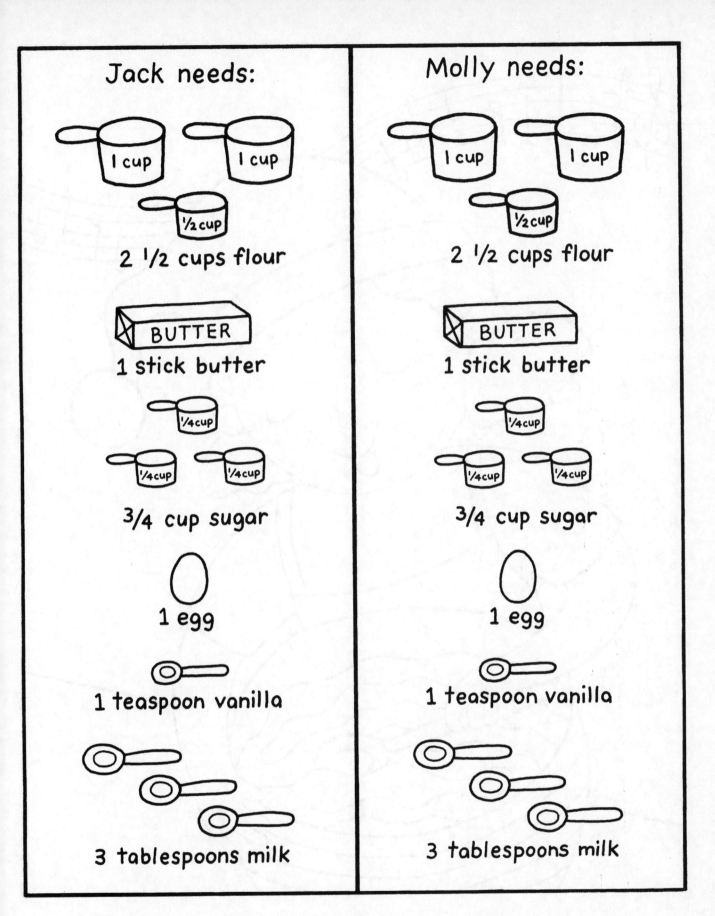

They will use double of everything. They count and measure.
How much do they need all together? 5 cups flour, 2 sticks butter,
1½ cups sugar, 2 eggs, 2 teaspoons vanilla, 6 tablespoons milk.

They mix their cookie dough. Then they form the dough into balls
that they put into the refrigerator to harden just a bit.

74

Christmas music is playing on the radio and they sing along.

Molly and Jack roll out the dough.

They cut out shapes with cookie cutters.

The cookies are ready to bake.

Grandma helps Jack and Molly put them into the hot oven.

Out they come, nicely browned. What a delicious smell!

1
Santa Claus

2
Christmas Wreaths

3
Doves

4
Gingerbread Men

5
Christmas Stockings

6
Christmas Trees

7
Reindeer

8
Mittens

9
Candycanes

10
Angels

11
Bells

12
Stars

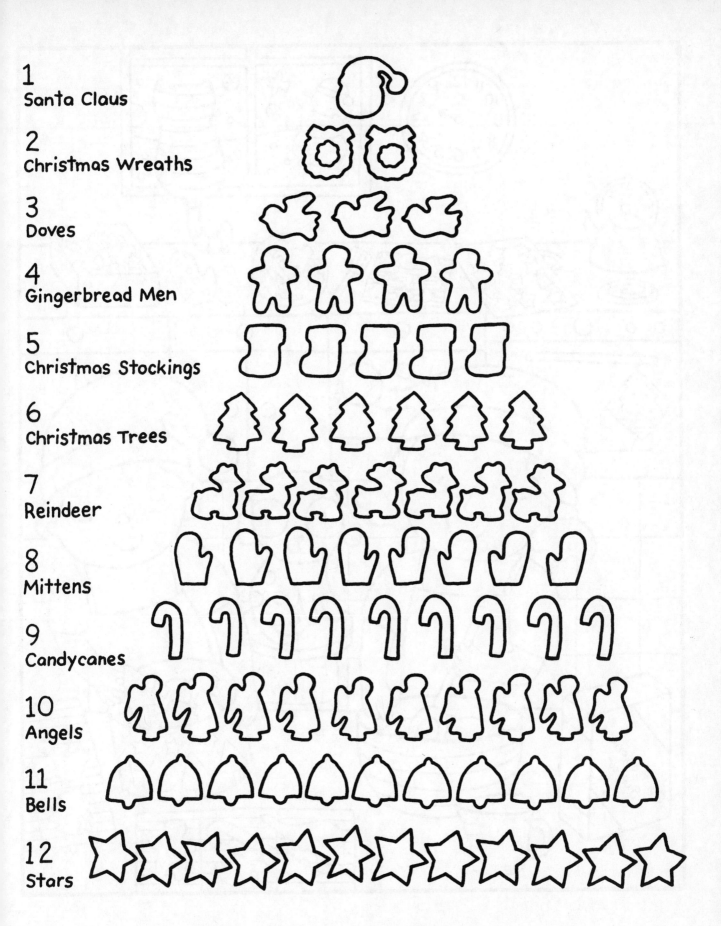

Look at all the cookies that are coming out of the oven!
Can you count them?

Molly makes the frosting while Jack gets the cookies ready for decorating.

82

RED for
candycane stripes

GREEN for
Christmas tree

YELLOW for
star

BLUE for
bird

PINK for
angel

ORANGE for
gingerbread man

They get out colored sprinkles. Each color goes into a different bowl.

They carefully decorate the cookies. First they spread on the frosting.

Then they decorate the cookies with the colored sprinkles.
What beautiful cookies!

They make cookies in lots of Christmas shapes. You can decorate them, too:
star, candycane, Christmas tree, reindeer, candle, Santa, stocking, flying angel,
mitten, holly leaf, snowflake, Nutcracker, snowman, gingerbread man,
trumpet, bell, dove, wreath, angel.

They also make cookies in lots of other fun shapes. Can you decorate these, too?
heart, dinosaur, duck, giraffe, rabbit, tulip, lion, fish, elephant, butterfly, airplane,
sailboat, rooster, ballerina, violin, ship, moon, cat, dog, car, ice cream cone

Jack and Molly show off their beautiful cookies. They are proud!

They share them with Mom and Dad, and Grandma and Grandpa.
Hurrah—Christmas is coming!

They pack up boxes of cookies.

They wrap them to give as presents to their friends.
So many things to do to get ready for Christmas!

They make a special plate of cookies for Santa.

At last, a cookie for Molly and Jack. Now everything is ready for Christmas!

MOLLY AND JACK'S
CHRISTMAS SUGAR COOKIES

2½ cups all-purpose flour
1 teaspoon baking powder
¼ teaspoon salt
½ cup butter

¾ cup sugar
1 egg
1 teaspoon vanilla extract
3 tablespoons milk

1. Mix together 2 cups of the flour, the baking powder, and salt. Set aside.

2. Cream together the butter and sugar. Then beat in the egg, vanilla extract, and milk.

3. Stir in the flour mixture, and then gradually add enough of the remaining flour to make the dough stiff enough to roll out.

4. Form the dough into 2 or 3 balls. Chill for at least 1 hour.

5. Preheat oven to 375 degrees.

6. Place the dough on a floured surface and roll out to about ¼-inch thick. Cut with cookie cutters and place on ungreased cookie sheets.

7. Bake about 8 to 10 minutes or until golden brown.
   (Makes about 4 dozen cookies.)

FROSTING

2 tablespoons butter
2 cups confectioners sugar
1 teaspoon vanilla extract
5 tablespoons milk (approximate)
Colored sprinkles

1. Cream together the butter, sugar, and vanilla extract.

2. Stir in 3 tablespoons of the milk. Gradually add enough of the remaining milk to make the frosting smooth and easy to spread.

3. Spread the frosting on cookies with a smooth-edged knife, and then decorate with colored sprinkles. Make the cookies colorful and have FUN!

MOLLY AND JACK'S
GINGERBREAD COOKIES

3 cups all-purpose flour
1 teaspoon baking soda
½ teaspoon salt
2 teaspoons ginger
2 teaspoons cinnamon
¼ teaspoon nutmeg

¼ teaspoon cloves
½ cup butter
½ cup brown sugar
½ cup molasses
1 egg

1. Mix together flour, baking soda, salt, and spices.
   Set aside.

2. Cream together the butter, brown sugar, and molasses.
   Then beat in the egg.

3. Stir in the flour mixture, one cup at a time. The dough will be stiff.

4. Form the dough into 2 or 3 balls. Chill for at least 1 hour.

5. Preheat oven to 350 degrees.

6. Place the dough on a floured surface and roll out to about ¼-inch thick.
   Cut with cookie cutters and place on ungreased cookie sheets.

7. Bake about 10 to 12 minutes or until nicely brown and crisp
   at the edges.
   (Makes about 4 dozen cookies.)

Frost the Gingerbread Cookies with the same frosting and directions
as for Christmas Sugar Cookies. If desired, decorate them with raisins,
pieces of dried fruits, and nuts.

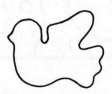

Shh . . . Santa is coming. Merry Christmas!

Christmas
Find & Color

Agostino Traini

Instructions

The Christmas scenes on the following pages all contain a series of boxes that show you exactly what to look for. Just draw a box around each "little picture" in the scene—and remember, if you get stuck, solutions can be found beginning on page 136.

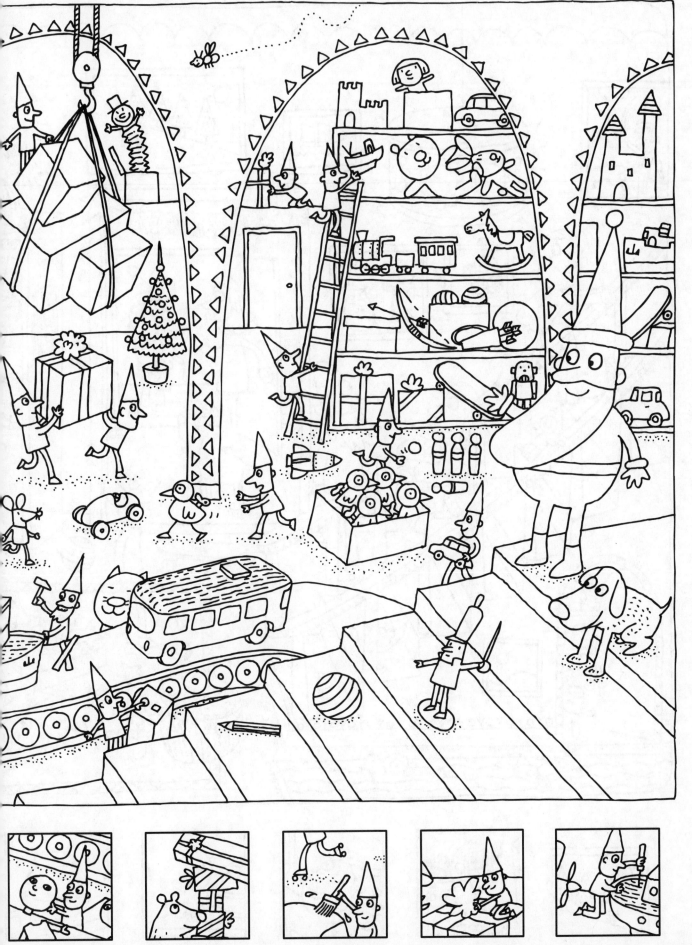

113

RAIL

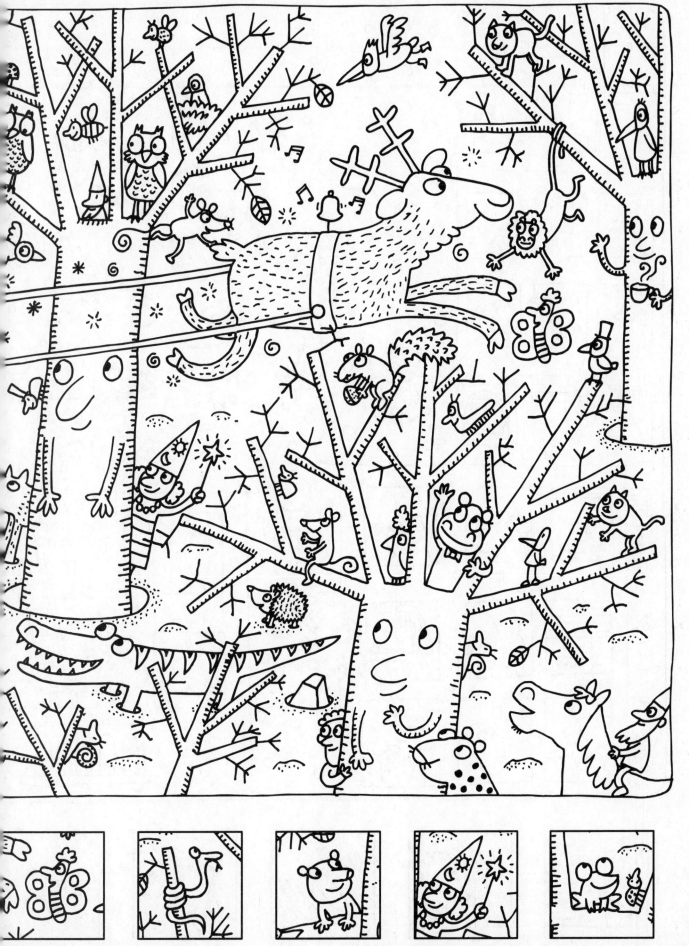

125

129

Solutions

Pages 100-101

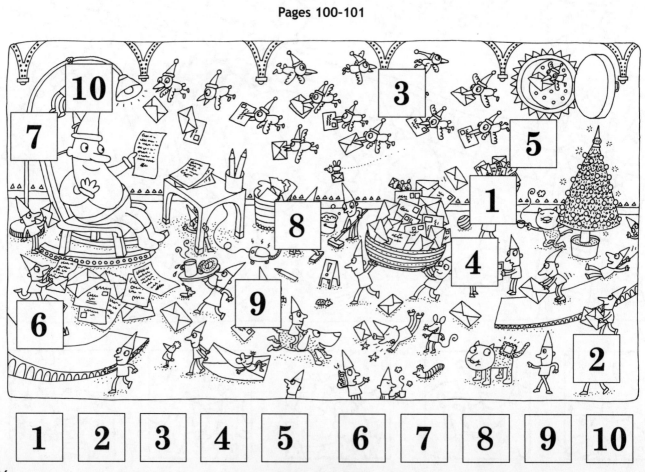

Pages 102-103

| 1 | 2 | 3 | 4 | 5 | 6 | 7 | 8 | 9 | 10 |

Pages 104-105

| 1 | 2 | 3 | 4 | 5 | 6 | 7 | 8 | 9 | 10 |

Pages 106-107

137

1 2 3 4 5 6 7 8 9 10

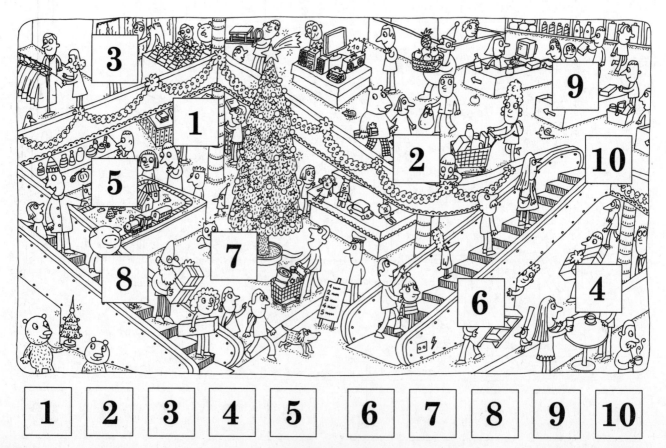

1 2 3 4 5 6 7 8 9 10

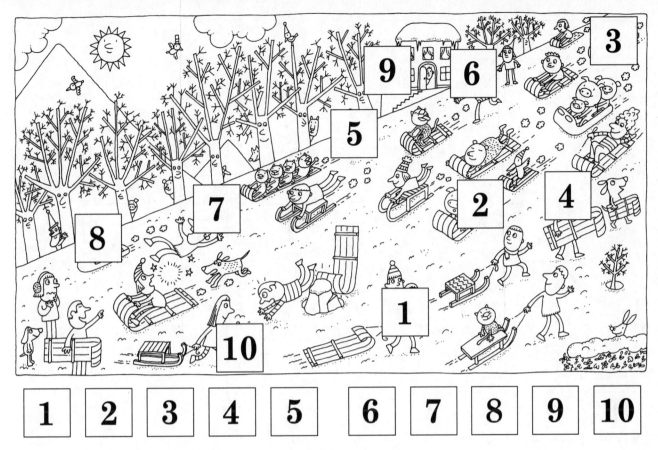

Pages 112-113

Pages 114-115

| 1 | 2 | 3 | 4 | 5 | 6 | 7 | 8 | 9 | 10 |

Pages 116-117

| 1 | 2 | 3 | 4 | 5 | 6 | 7 | 8 | 9 | 10 |

Pages 118-119

Pages 120-121

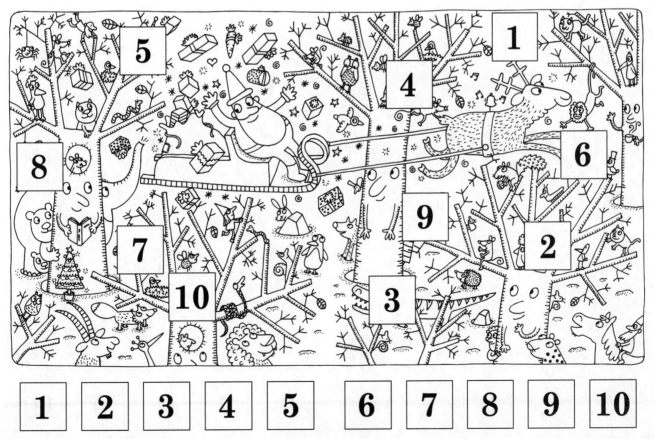

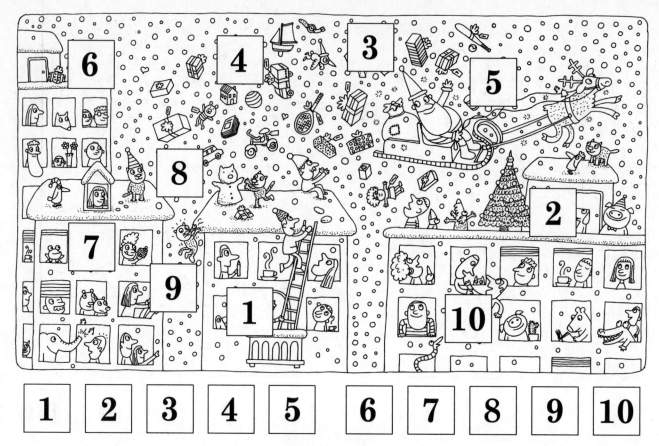

| 1 | 2 | 3 | 4 | 5 | 6 | 7 | 8 | 9 | 10 |

Pages 128-129

| 1 | 2 | 3 | 4 | 5 | 6 | 7 | 8 | 9 | 10 |

1 2 3 4 5 6 7 8 9 10

Pages 132-133

1 2 3 4 5 6 7 8 9 10

Pages 134-135

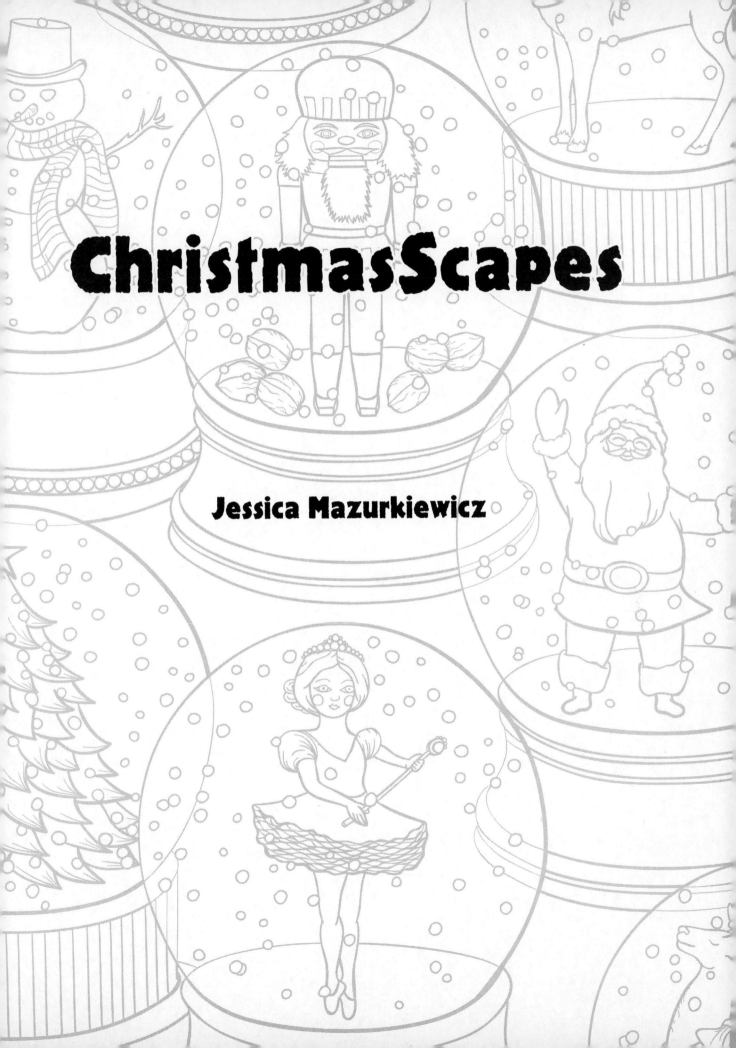

ChristmasScapes

Jessica Mazurkiewicz

147

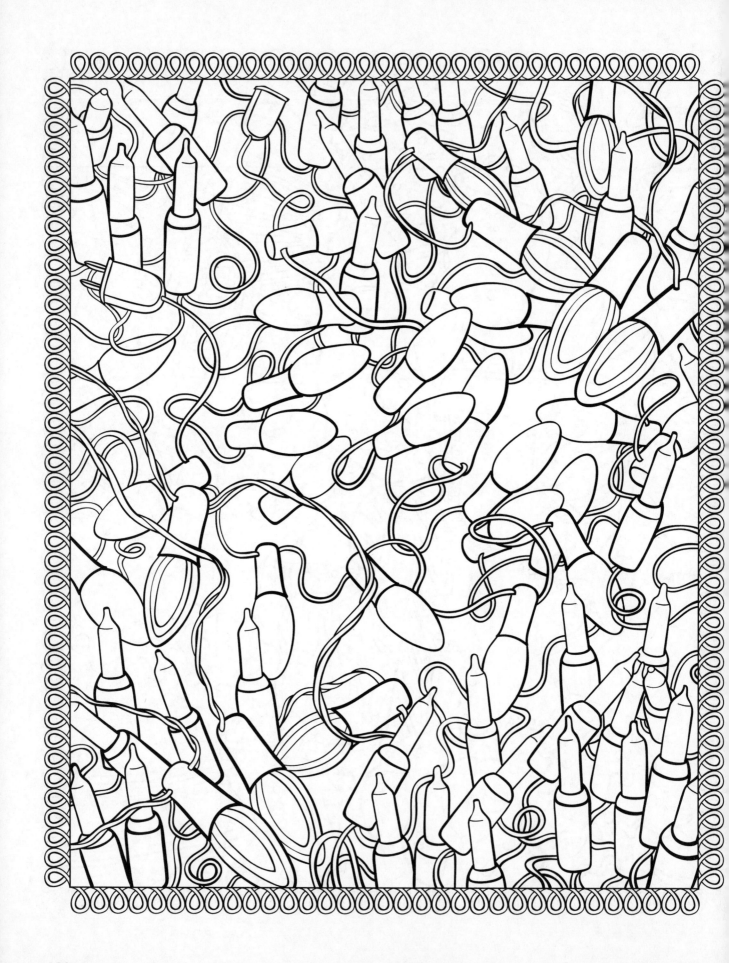

153

154

157

159

160

164

165

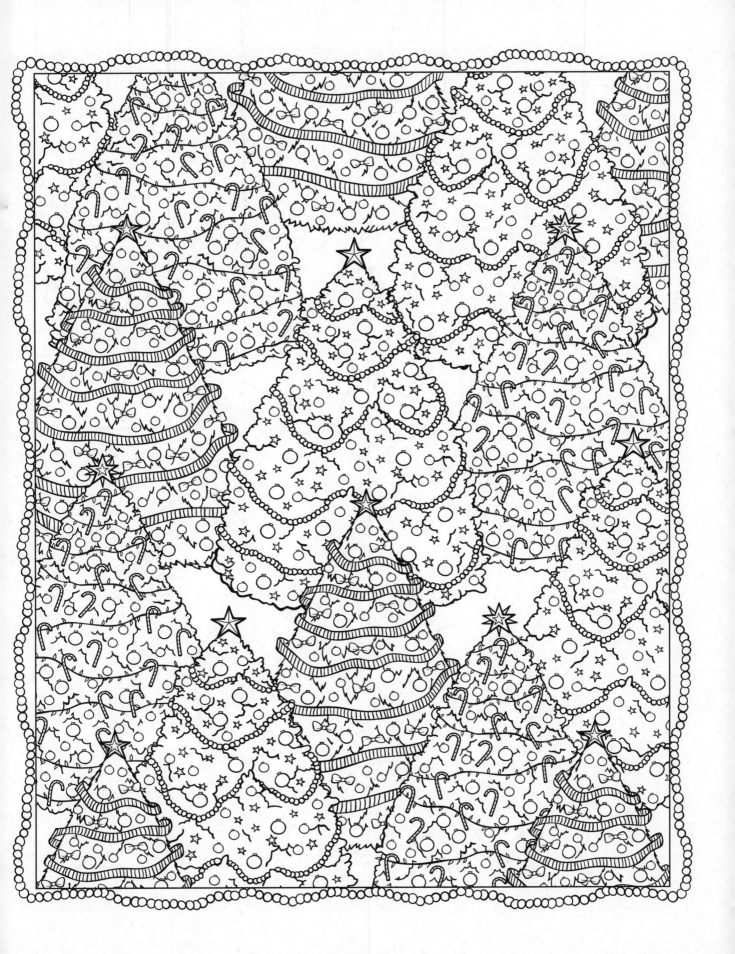

167

169

173

174

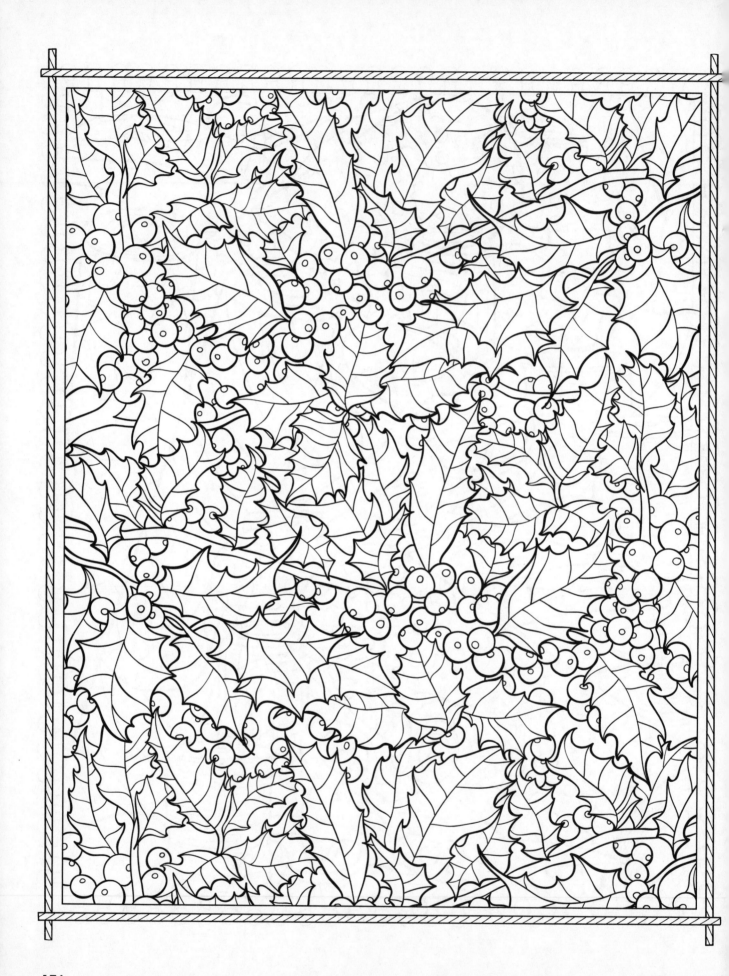

Christmas Family Fun

COLORING BOOK

Cathy Beylon

Christmas is coming! Ben and Emmie are
counting the days till December 25th!

Mom has been out Christmas shopping.
Look at all the packages!

Ben and Emmie are helping Mom put up
Christmas decorations.

It's snowing! Let's help Daddy build a snowman!

All aboard for a sleigh ride down the hill! Whoopee!

OUTSIDE
CHRISTMAS
LIGHTS

184

It's time to help Daddy put up the
Christmas lights. What fun!

We're off to the tree farm to find
a beautiful Christmas tree!

How about this one?
The whole family likes this tree.

Everybody helps decorate the tree with ornaments, candy canes, and snowmen—and on top, a beautiful star!

Ben and Emmie are writing letters to Santa Claus.
Have *you* been good this year?

Let's put on our Christmas hats!
Just like the one Santa wears!

Santa's visiting the mall.

Now Ben and Emmie can tell him
what they want for Christmas.

Mommy's writing Christmas cards to friends and relatives.

Even Kirby the dog is decorated for
Christmas—with reindeer antlers!

At Christmas time, people go from
house to house singing carols.

The mailbox is full of Christmas cards and packages.

Mom and Dad are making Christmas cookies. Yummy!

The whole family is decorating the house for
Christmas—even little Nate wants to help.

The stockings are hung by the chimney with care.
Don't forget Kirby!

It's time to wrap Christmas presents!
Who wants to help?

It's the night before Christmas—
time to put the presents under the tree.

Ben, Emmie, and Nate are leaving milk and cookies for Santa.
Hope Santa's hungry!

Soon it will be bedtime. Daddy reads
The Night Before Christmas.

Santa's here with his big bag of toys.
Lots of treats for good girls and boys!

Christmas morning at last!
Look at all the presents!

Ben, Emmie, and Nate love their new toys.
Even Kirby got a gift! Merry Christmas to everybody!

How to Draw
Christmas Pictures

Barbara Soloff Levy

Instructions

To draw the Christmas pictures on the following pages, you will follow four steps. First, in step one, draw the basic shapes of the picture shown on the page. Then, in steps two and three, you will add details. In step four, you will complete your picture and add shading to make it look even better.

You may want to trace the steps of each picture first, just to get the feel of the drawing. Then you can begin work on your picture, drawing on the practice pages provided for you in this book, or in a sketchbook of your own. Make sure to use a pencil in case you decide to make changes. Some of the pictures have dotted lines—erase these lines as a final step. When you are happy with your drawing, go over the lines with a felt tip pen or a colored pencil, and finally, go ahead and color your drawing any way you like.

Practice Page

Practice Page

216 Mrs. Claus

Practice Page

Practice Page

Practice Page

Practice Page

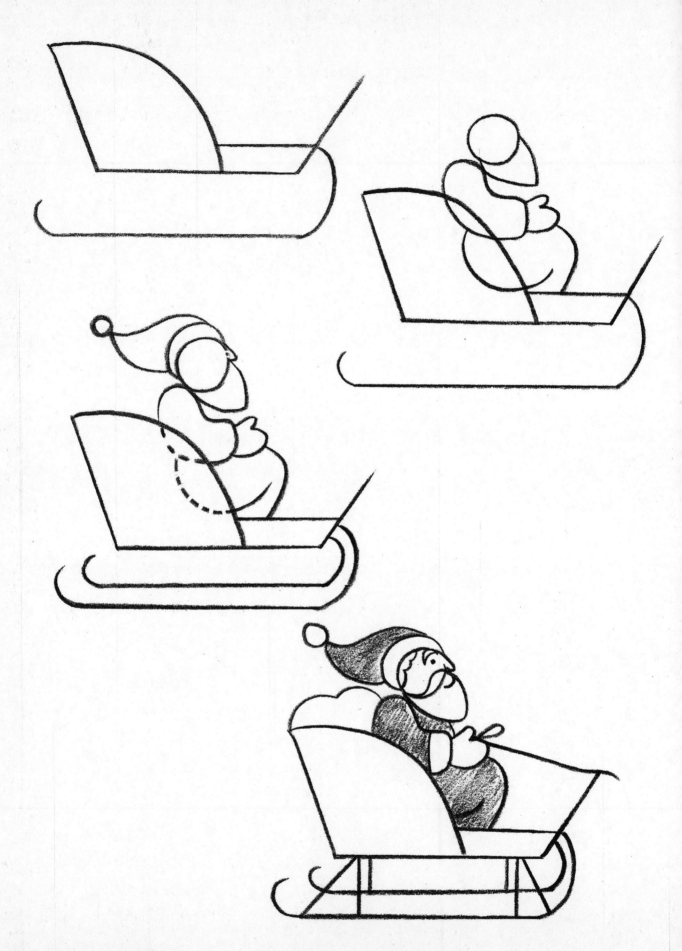

Practice Page

Practice Page

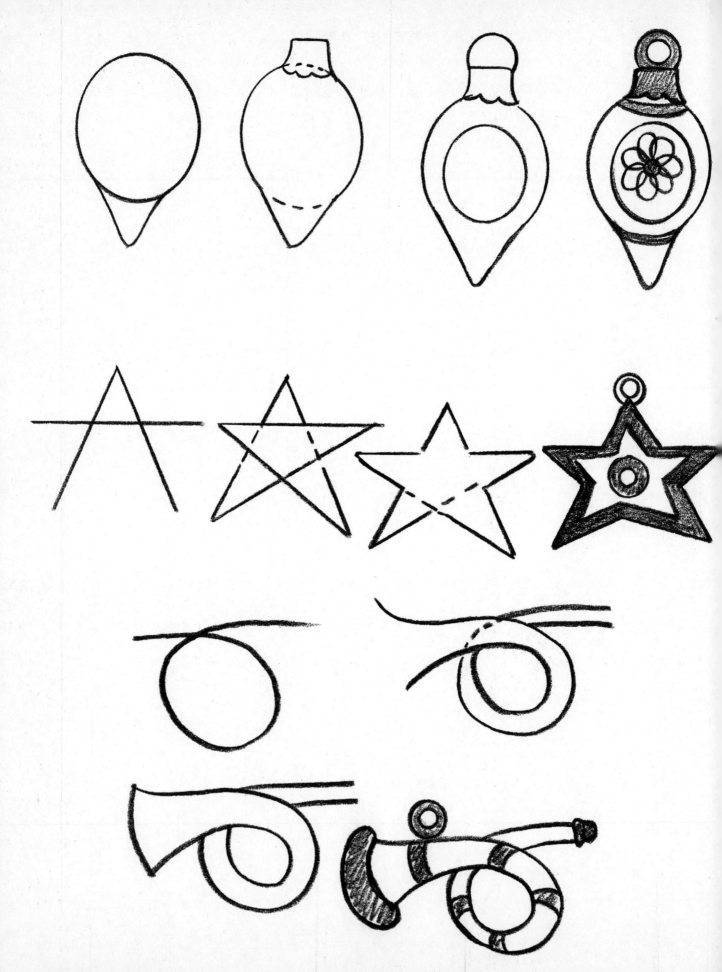

Practice Page

Practice Page

Practice Page

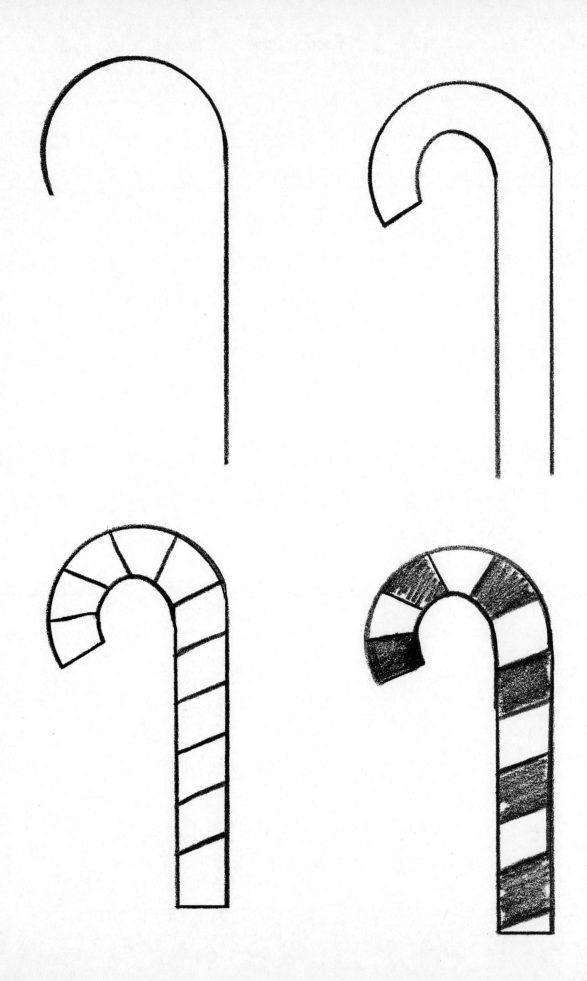

Practice Page

238   Poinsettia

Practice Page

240 Wreath

Practice Page

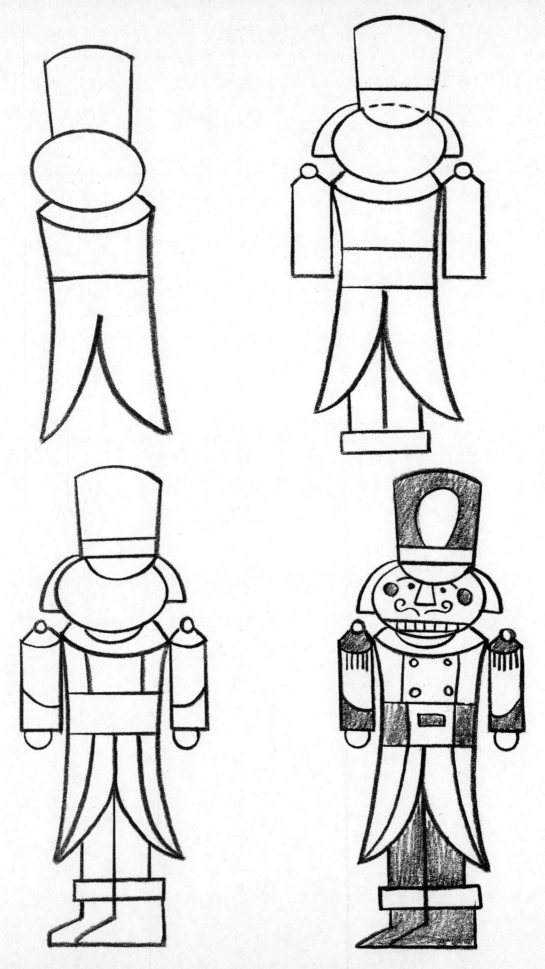

242 Nutcracker Toy Soldier

Practice Page

244 Christmas Bells

Practice Page

246 Dove

Practice Page

Practice Page

Practice Page

Practice Page

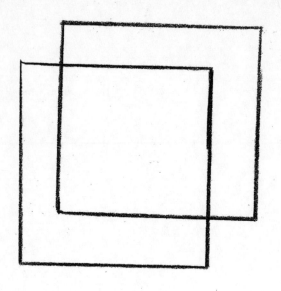

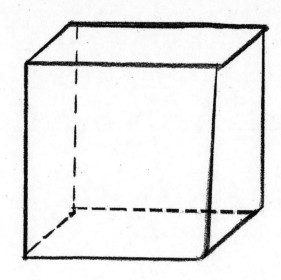

Practice Page

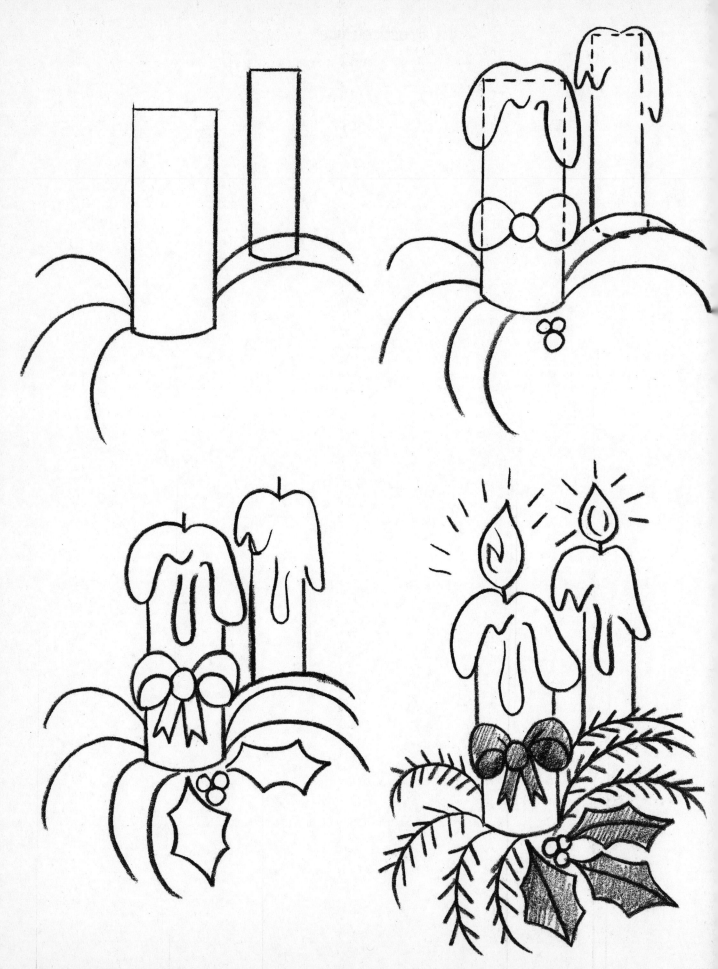

Practice Page

Practice Page

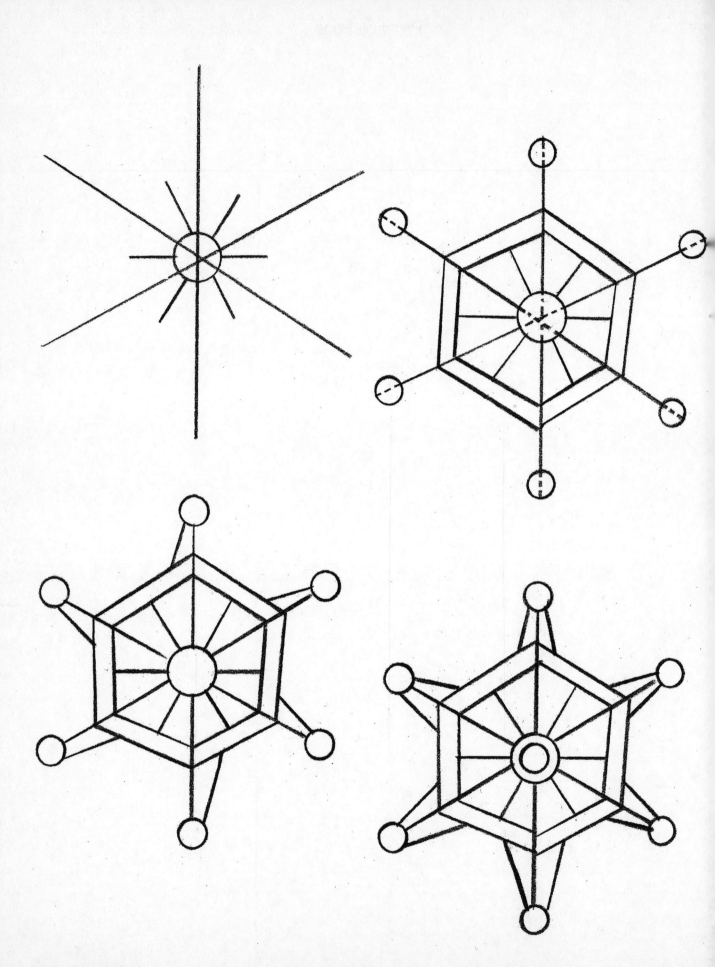

Practice Page

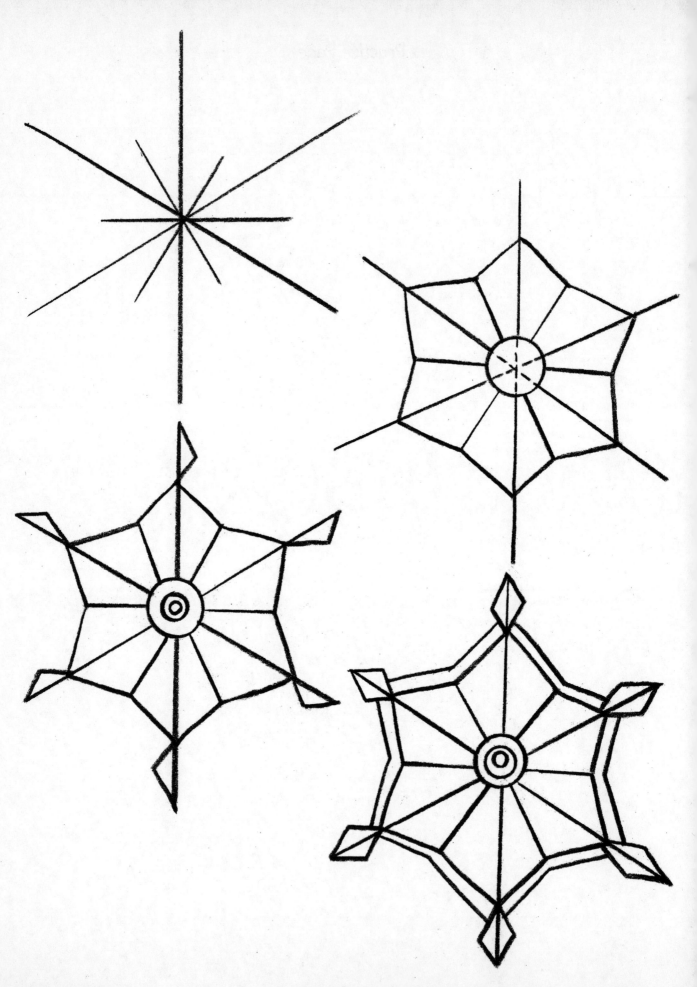

Practice Page

266   Child on a Sled

Practice Page

Practice Page